To My Child

A Mother's Journal

PAINTINGS BY
Sandra Kuck

Harvest House Publishers
Eugene, Oregon 97402

To My Child

Copyright © 1997 Harvest House Publishers
Eugene, Oregon 97402

ISBN 1-56507-607-9

All works of art in this book are copyrighted by Sandra Kuck and may not be reproduced without permission. For information regarding art in this book, please contact:

V.F. Fine Arts, Inc.
1737 Stibbens, #240B
Houston, TX 77043

Design and production by Garborg Design Works, Minneapolis, Minnesota

Harvest House Publishers has made every effort to trace the ownership of all quotes and poems in this book. In the event of any question arising from the use of a quote or poem, we regret any error made and will be pleased to make the necessary correction in future editions of this book.

All rights reserved. No portion of this book may be reproduced in any form without the written permission of the Publisher.

Printed in United States of America.

97 98 99 00 01 02 03 04 05 06 /WZ/ 10 9 8 7 6 5 4 3

To My Child

You are precious to me, dear child.
And so I've kept this journal to
celebrate memories—memories of you
and me and the many special people,
places, and events that have shaped
your life and made you the wonderful
person you are today.

I've written this journal with love,
and I've filled it with stories and
feelings I hope you will cherish.
Many things in life fade away, but
love and memories remain. When
you read this, know that your mother
loves you and remembers you...always.

The experiences
you have had
are your own
greatest treasure,
well worth the
remembering
and retelling.

Ray Mungo

From My Heart
to Yours

Contents

Our Family Tree

Grandmother

Mother

Grandfather

You

Grandmother

Father

Grandfather

Great Grandmother

Great Grandfather

Great Grandmother

Great Grandfather

Great Grandmother

Great Grandfather

Great Grandmother

Great Grandfather

*Like branches on a
tree, we may grow in
different directions,*

*Yet our roots remain
as one.*

*Each of our lives will
always be a special
part*

Of the other.

Your Maternal Grandparents

(PLACE PHOTO HERE.)

Her Maiden Name

_____

Her Birth Date

_____

Place of Birth

_____

His Name

_____

His Birth Date

_____

Place of Birth

_____

Your grandmother's best stories of growing up _____

_____

_____

_____

_____

_____

_____

Her education and life's work _____

_____

_____

_____

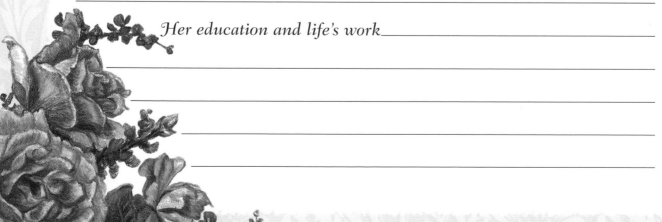

What she valued most in life _____
_____
_____
_____
_____
_____

Your grandfather's best stories of growing up _____
_____
_____
_____
_____
_____

His education and life's work _____
_____
_____
_____
_____
_____

What he valued most in life _____
_____
_____
_____

They met _____

_____

_____

They were married _____

Memories they shared of their wedding and honeymoon _____

_____

_____

_____

_____

Their first home _____

_____

They loved to spend time together _____

_____

_____

_____

_____

Favorite stories about their years together _____

_____

_____

_____

_____

_____

_____

What I want you to know about your maternal grandparents

_____

_____

_____

_____

_____

_____

_____

_____

_____

_____

_____

_____

_____

How you remind me of them _____

_____

_____

_____

_____

_____

Your Grandmother's Favorites

Color _____ Flower _____ Fragrance _____

Book/Author _____

Music _____

Movie/Actor _____

Things to wear _____

_____

Things to do on a rainy day _____

_____

Things to do on a sunny day _____

_____

Place _____

Poem/Verse _____

_____

_____

_____

Meal/Recipe _____

_____

_____

Other favorites _____

_____

All that I am
or hope to be
I owe to my
angel mother.
Abraham Lincoln

Your Grandfather's Favorites

Color _____ Hobby _____ Sport _____

Book/Author _____

Music _____

Movie/Actor _____

Things to wear _____

_____

Things to do on a rainy day _____

_____

Things to do on a sunny day _____

_____

Place _____

Poem/Verse _____

_____

_____

_____

Meal/Recipe _____

_____

_____

_____

Other favorites _____

_____

_____

Loving Your Grandmother

Your grandmother is special to me because _____

_____

_____

_____

She taught me so much about _____

_____

_____

_____

_____

I'll always remember the time we _____

_____

_____

_____

What I learned about being a good wife and mother from her example ____

_____

_____

_____

When I think of her, I'll always remember _____

_____

_____

_____

Loving Your Grandfather

Your grandfather is special to me because _____

_____

_____

_____

He taught me so much about _____

_____

_____

_____

I'll always remember the time we _____

_____

_____

What I learned about husbands and fathers from his example _____

_____

_____

_____

When I think of him, I'll always remember _____

_____

_____

_____

_____

Your Paternal Grandparents

Her Maiden Name

_____

Her Birth Date

_____

Place of Birth

_____

His Name

_____

His Birth Date

_____

Place of Birth

_____

(PLACE PHOTO HERE.)

Your grandmother's best stories of growing up _____

_____

_____

_____

_____

_____

_____

Her education and life's work _____

_____

_____

_____

_____

What she valued most in life _____

_____

_____

_____

_____

_____

Your grandfather's best stories of growing up _____

_____

_____

_____

_____

_____

His education and life's work _____

_____

_____

_____

_____

_____

What he valued most in life _____

_____

_____

_____

_____

They met _____

_____

_____

They were married _____

Memories they shared of their wedding and honeymoon _____

_____

_____

_____

_____

Their first home _____

_____

They loved to spend time together _____

_____

_____

_____

_____

Favorite stories about their years together _____

_____

_____

_____

_____

_____

_____

What I want you to know about your paternal grandparents _____

_____

_____

_____

_____

_____

_____

_____

_____

_____

_____

_____

_____

_____

How you remind me of them _____

_____

_____

_____

_____

_____

May the Lord
continually bless
you with heaven's
blessings…
May you live
to enjoy your
grandchildren!

The Book of Psalms

Your Grandmother's Favorites

Color _____ Flower _____ Fragrance _____

Book/Author _____

Music _____

Movie/Actor _____

Things to wear _____

_____

Things to do on a rainy day _____

_____

Things to do on a sunny day _____

_____

Place _____

Poem/Verse _____

_____

_____

_____

Meal/Recipe _____

_____

_____

Other favorites _____

_____

_____

Her children stand and bless her, so does her husband. He praises her with these words, "There are many fine women in the world, but you are the best of them all!"

The Book of Proverbs

20

Your Grandfather's Favorites

Color_____ Hobby_____ Sport_____

Book/Author_____

Music_____

Movie/Actor_____

Things to wear_____

_____

Things to do on a rainy day_____

_____

Things to do on a sunny day_____

_____

Place_____

Poem/Verse_____

_____

_____

_____

Meal/Recipe_____

_____

_____

_____

Other favorites_____

_____

_____

Loving Your Grandmother

Your grandmother is special to your dad because _____
_____
_____
_____

She taught him so much about _____
_____
_____
_____
_____

He'll always remember the time they _____
_____
_____
_____

What your dad learned about wives and mothers from her example _____
_____
_____
_____

When Dad thinks of her, he'll always remember _____
_____
_____
_____

Loving Your Grandfather

Your grandfather is special to your dad because _____

_____

_____

_____

He taught him so much about _____

_____

_____

_____

> The most important thing a father can do for his children is to love their mother.

He'll always remember the time they _____

_____

_____

_____

What your dad learned about being a good husband and father from his example

_____

_____

_____

When Dad thinks of him, he'll always remember _____

_____

_____

_____

_____

All About Me

(PLACE PHOTO HERE.)

Maiden Name

_____

My Birth Date

_____

Place of Birth

_____

When I was young, I was called _____

One childhood story that has been told many times _____

_____

_____

Memories of where I lived _____

_____

_____

_____

What I loved about growing up with my siblings _____

_____

_____

My favorite times with my family were _____

_____

_____

_____

My childhood friends and I loved to _____

_____

The schools I attended were _____

_____

In school I was really great in _____

    but I found it harder to _____

_____

School activities I enjoyed were _____

_____

When I was young, I dreamed of _____

_____

They always looked back before turning the corner, for their mother was always at the window to nod and smile, and wave her hand at them. Somehow it seemed as if they couldn't have got through the day without that, for whatever their mood might be, the last glimpse of that motherly face was sure to affect them like sunshine.

Louisa May Alcott
LITTLE WOMEN

My Childhood Favorites

I loved to eat _____

I enjoyed reading _____

Songs I remember best are _____

Television shows I never missed _____

The movies I enjoyed most were _____

I really loved wearing _____

Things to do on a rainy day _____

_____

Things to do on a sunny day _____

_____

Toys I cherished _____

Places I played _____

People I looked up to _____

Places to go with my family _____

_____

Other childhood favorites _____

_____

_____

_____

_____

Recall as often
as you wish;
a happy memory
never wears out.

Libbie Fudim

Growing Up

Memories of my first date or dance _____

_____

_____

_____

The first time I thought I was in love _____

_____

_____

_____

In high school I was involved in _____

_____

_____

_____

_____

My best friend in high school was _____

    and we loved to _____

_____

_____

_____

_____

_____

Ways I earned money _____

_____

_____

The popular fashions and fads were _____

_____

_____

Significant national and world events _____

_____

_____

_____

After high school I _____

_____

_____

_____

My first job _____

Other memories of my young adult life _____

_____

_____

_____

_____

_____

All About Your Father

(PLACE PHOTO HERE.)

His Birth Date

_____

Place of Birth

_____

When he was young, he was called _____

One childhood story that has been told many times _____

_____

_____

Memories of where he lived _____

_____

_____

_____

What he loved about growing up with his siblings _____

_____

_____

His favorite times with his family were _____

_____

_____

_____

He and his childhood friends loved to _____

_____

The schools he attended were _____

_____

In school he was really great in _____

but he found it harder to _____

_____

School activities he enjoyed were _____

_____

When he was young, he dreamed of _____

_____

_____

Your Father's Childhood Favorites

He loved to eat _____

He enjoyed reading _____

Sports he loved playing _____

Television shows he never missed _____

The movies he enjoyed most were _____

He really loved wearing _____

Things to do on a rainy day _____

_____

Things to do on a sunny day _____

_____

Toys he cherished _____

Places he played _____

People he looked up to _____

Places to go with his family _____

_____

Other childhood favorites _____

_____

_____

_____

_____

His Growing Up

Memories of his first date or dance _____
_____
_____
_____

The first time he thought he was in love _____
_____
_____
_____

In high school he was involved in _____
_____
_____
_____
_____

His best friend in high school was_____
    and they loved to _____
_____
_____
_____
_____
_____

Do not delay;
the golden
memories fly!

*Henry Wadsworth
Longfellow*

Ways he earned money _____

_____

_____

The popular fashions and fads were _____

_____

_____

Significant national and world events _____

_____

_____

_____

After high school he _____

_____

_____

_____

His first job _____

Other memories of his young adult life _____

_____

_____

_____

_____

_____

When I First Loved Your Father

Your father and I met _____

_____

_____

My first impression of him _____

_____

His first impression of me _____

_____

Things we liked to do _____

_____

_____

_____

How your father proposed to me _____

_____

_____

How I accepted his proposal _____

_____

The first people we told of our engagement _____

_____

Your father and I were married on _____

    at _____

    ceremony performed by _____

The bridal party included _____

_____

My most vivid memory of our wedding day _____

_____

_____

_____

The funniest thing that happened on our wedding day _____

_____

_____

Our honeymoon memories include _____

_____

_____

One thing that surprised me about marriage _____

_____

What I most want you to know about marriage _____

_____

_____

Love always
protects, always
trusts, always
hopes, always
perseveres. Love
never fails.

1 Corinthians 13

_____

_____

_____

_____

Our New Life Together

Our first home was _____

_____

As newlyweds, your father and I spent a lot of time _____

_____

_____

_____

_____

_____

Dear friends at that time were _____

_____

_____

_____

Your father worked at _____

I worked at _____

Significant national and world events that affected us _____

_____

_____

_____

_____

*Our plans and dreams as a young couple*_____

_____

_____

_____

_____

_____

_____

_____

_____

*Other reflections of our early years together*_____

_____

_____

_____

_____

Home is the one
place in all the
world where
hearts are sure
of each other.

*Frederick W.
Robertson*

_____

_____

_____

My Favorites

Color _____ Flower _____ Fragrance _____

Book/Author _____

Music _____

Movie/Actor _____

Things to wear _____

_____

Things to do on a rainy day _____

_____

Things to do on a sunny day _____

_____

Place _____

Poem/Verse _____

_____

_____

_____

Meal/Recipe _____

_____

_____

Other favorites _____

_____

_____

Your Father's Favorites

Color _____ Hobby _____ Sport _____

Book/Author _____

Music _____

Movie/Actor _____

Things to wear _____

_____

Things to do on a rainy day _____

_____

Things to do on a sunny day _____

_____

Place _____

Poem/Verse _____

_____

_____

_____

Meal/Recipe _____

_____

_____

_____

Other favorites _____

_____

_____

My Little Miracle

The day I learned I was expecting you, I _____

_____

_____

_____

When I told your father, he _____

_____

_____

_____

_____

To prepare for you, we _____

_____

_____

_____

_____

While I was in labor, your father _____

_____

_____

_____

_____

You arrived at _____ at _____ hospital.

When I first saw you, I_____

_____

_____

When your father first saw you, he_____

_____

_____

The moment I first held you, I felt_____

_____

_____

We chose your name because_____

_____

_____

When the rest of the family heard of your arrival, they_____

_____

_____

Other cherished sentiments_____

_____

_____

_____

_____

_____

In the sheltered
simplicity of the first
days after a baby is
born, one sees again
the magical closed
circle, the miraculous
sense of two people
existing only for
each other.

Anne Morrow Lindbergh

With Love from Mom

_____

_____

_____

_____

_____

_____

_____

_____

_____

_____

_____

_____

_____

_____

_____

With Love from Dad

Tender Moments of
Your First Four Years

As a baby, you were _____
_____
_____
_____
_____

One thing your father and I would do to stop you from crying was _____
_____
_____

An object that you became very attached to_____
_____

Once you could walk, you loved to _____
_____
_____

The most surprising thing you did as a toddler was_____
_____
_____
_____
_____
_____

Things you did that made people smile _____

_____

_____

At bedtime, you _____

_____

_____

Your personality was _____

_____

Teach a child to choose the right path, and when he's older he will remain upon it.

The Book of Proverbs

_____

Your first gift to me _____

_____

_____

Some of my favorite memories of you as a toddler _____

_____

_____

_____

_____

_____

_____

_____

_____

_____

_____

School Days

Your first school was _____

On your first day of school, I felt _____

_____

_____

_____

Your first impressions of school were _____

_____

Your teacher said _____

_____

During elementary school, you really enjoyed _____

_____

Your favorite teachers were _____

_____

_____

I'll never forget when you _____

_____

_____

Other wonderful memories _____

_____

_____

_____

Your Childhood Favorites

You loved to eat _____

You enjoyed reading _____

A song we loved to sing together _____

Television shows you never missed _____

Movies you enjoyed _____

You were always wearing _____

Things you did on rainy days _____

_____

Things you did on sunny days _____

_____

Toys you cherished _____

_____

Places you went _____

_____

Animals you liked _____

Games and sports you played _____

_____

Your hero was _____

Other special favorites _____

_____

_____

A Time Remembered

On your first day of middle school, I could tell _____
_____

Your attitudes about school at the time were _____
_____

I enjoyed watching you excel in _____
_____

Other activities I was proud you were involved in _____
_____

The day you became a teenager, I felt _____
_____
_____

I noticed our relationship changed in these ways _____
_____
_____

What you said you wanted to be when you grew up _____
_____

Other unforgettable memories about this time in your life _____
_____
_____
_____
_____

A Circle of Friends

I remember your first "best friend" _____

_____

Special friends of yours I really liked _____

_____

You and your friends seemed to love to _____

_____

_____

I'll never forget when you and your friends _____

_____

_____

_____

I think you make a good friend because _____

_____

_____

_____

_____

_____

_____

_____

_____

> We have only this moment, sparkling like a star in our hand—and melting like a snowflake.
>
> *Marie Beynon Ray*

Pathway of Promise

One thing I'll always remember about your high school years _____

_____

_____

I enjoyed watching your involvement in _____

_____

I was so proud of you when _____

_____

_____

The first time you earned your own money, I knew _____

_____

_____

The day you got your driver's license, I _____

_____

I remember your first date _____

_____

_____

_____

When you had your first "serious" relationship, I _____

_____

_____

_____

What you talked about becoming _____

_____

_____

After high school you planned _____

_____

_____

As you prepared for your future, I hoped _____

_____

_____

_____

On your graduation day, I felt _____

_____

_____

_____

Our relationship had become _____

_____

_____

Other outstanding memories about this time in your life _____

_____

_____

_____

_____

> May wisdom and truth enter the center of your being, filling your life with joy.
>
> *The Book of Proverbs*

Our Family... A Circle of Strength

In our family, you were always the one_____

_____

_____

What makes you different from your siblings_____

_____

_____

_____

My most vivid memory of you and your siblings_____

_____

_____

_____

How you're like me_____

_____

_____

_____

_____

How you're like your father_____

_____

_____

_____

You resemble _____

_____

_____

_____

What everyone in the family appreciates most about you _____

_____

_____

_____

_____

_____

Family times I'll always remember _____

_____

_____

_____

_____

_____

_____

_____

_____

_____

Good family life is never an accident but always an achievement by those who share it.

James Bossard

Warm Traditions and Family Celebrations

Your favorite holiday has always been _____

What I treasure about our family celebrations _____

_____

_____

_____

_____

In my mind, our most important family tradition is _____

_____

_____

_____

_____

Other precious holiday memories _____

_____

_____

_____

_____

_____

_____

Joy in the Journey

One of our best trips as a family was _____

_____

_____

_____

_____

The first time you traveled without the family, I felt _____

_____

_____

_____

Some of my fondest recollections of you on vacation _____

_____

_____

_____

_____

_____

_____

_____

> Adventure is
> worthwhile
> in itself.
>
> *Amelia Earhart*

Golden Moments—
Favorite Photos of You

Each moment
is a place we've
never been.

Mark Strand

The happiest
moments of my
life have been the
few which I have
passed at home
in the bosom of
my family

Thomas Jefferson

All Grown Up

Your personality is_____
_____
_____

You laugh about_____
_____
_____

You're a softie when it comes to_____
_____
_____
_____

> Just as the ripe fruit breaks off from the tree, so a time will come when you will have to break off from your mother. It's sad…but it's something also to be glad about, since it means that you are growing up.
>
> *Isoka Hatano*
> (FROM A LETTER TO HER SON)

The hardest thing I have ever seen you go through_____
_____
_____
_____

Things that come easy to you are_____
_____
_____

You have very strong opinions about_____
_____
_____
_____

Your Love Story

When I first met the love of your life, I felt _____

_____

_____

_____

_____

When you announced your engagement, I thought _____

_____

_____

_____

_____

_____

My feelings on the day you were married _____

_____

_____

_____

_____

_____

_____

_____

_____

I love this about the person you married _____

_____

_____

_____

_____

_____

_____

_____

_____

Therefore a man is to leave his father and mother and he and his wife are united so that they are no longer two, but one.

The Book of Mark

If I could have one wish for your married life, it would be _____

_____

_____

_____

_____

_____

_____

_____

_____

_____

Private Thoughts

The guiding values and beliefs in my life are _____
_____
_____
_____
_____
_____
_____

The hardest thing I've ever had to do was _____
_____
_____
_____
_____
_____
_____

One of the happiest moments in my life was when _____
_____
_____
_____
_____
_____

My philosophy of life is _____

_____

_____

_____

_____

_____

If I could live my life over again, I might _____

_____

_____

_____

_____

_____

If I could change one aspect of being a mother to you, I _____

_____

_____

_____

_____

_____

From My Heart to Yours

You mean so much to me because _____
_____
_____
_____
_____
_____

How having you has changed my life _____
_____
_____
_____
_____

Being your mother has taught me _____
_____
_____
_____
_____

I have never felt closer to you than the time _____
_____
_____
_____

I am so proud of the way you _____

_____

_____

_____

_____

_____

I have always admired your _____

_____

_____

_____

_____

_____

I never told you, but _____

_____

_____

_____

_____

_____

I would like your children to know that you _____

_____

_____

_____

My Hope and Prayer for You

_____
_____
_____
_____
_____
_____
_____
_____
_____
_____
_____
_____
_____
_____
_____
_____
_____

Other Thoughts of Love

Sweet
memories
are treasured
heirlooms.

Treasured Keepsakes

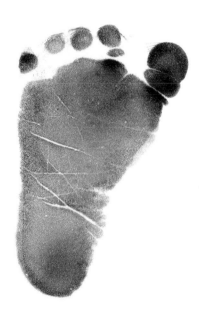

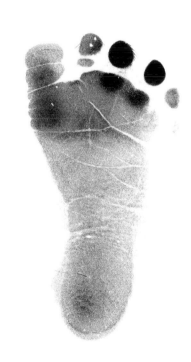

Happy times and
bygone days are
never lost...
in truth, they grow
more wonderful
within the heart
that keeps them.

Kay Andrew

When we do the
best we can, we
never know what
miracle is
wrought in our
life, or in the
life of another.

Helen Keller

The heart is like a
treasure chest
that's filled with
souvenirs. It's
there we keep the
memories we
gather through
the years.

Mothers hold
their children's
hands for just
a little while...
but their hearts
forever.